A Model for Effective School Discipline

by
Mildred Carter

Library of Congress Catalog Card Number 86-63884
ISBN 0-87367-250-X
Copyright © 1987 by the Phi Delta Kappa Educational Foundation
Bloomington, Indiana

This fastback is sponsored by the Toledo Ohio Chapter of Phi Delta Kappa, which made a generous contribution toward publication costs.

Table of Contents

Introduction 7
   What Is Discipline? 8

Prospect School: A Profile 11

Prospect School's Model for Effective Discipline 13

Prospect School's Discipline Program in Action 17
   Special Recognitions 19
   Recognition of Good Citizens 20
   Making Rules and Living by Them 22

Components of the Model 29
   A Shared Sense of Purpose for Discipline Training 29
   Focus on the Individual Student's Needs 30
   Purposeful and Organized Activity for Learning Self-Discipline .. 31
   Personal Responsibility for the Success of the Program 32

References 33

Introduction

According to the Gallup Poll of Public Attitudes Toward Education conducted each year for Phi Delta Kappa, first on the list of the most important problems facing the public schools from 1969 to 1985 was "lack of discipline." In 1986 discipline dropped to second place in the poll behind "use of drugs," which, in my opinion, also is a problem of discipline. Why has discipline persisted as a problem for nearly two decades? Baker (1985) argues that the persistence of discipline problems stems from several sources. For example:

1. Principals may ignore or play down the problem out of fear of appearing incompetent and unable to control their schools.

2. Many schools have failed to establish minimal procedures for dealing with discipline problems.

3. Many discipline actions are ineffective because they are inappropriate. For example, in one school 45% of all suspensions were for tardiness or skipping class.

4. A number of recent court decisions may have had a chilling effect on the willingness of school officials to enforce disciplinary standards. It is not clear whether school officials actually have been hampered by the court actions or whether they have failed to act because they believe that court decisions prevent them from acting.

Heading the list of underlying causes of discipline problems are inadequate parenting, ineffective teacher training, poor school organization, and inadequate administrative leadership. Other causes cited include inappropriate curricula; severe behavioral or learning disorders exacerbated by certain school environments; poor self-esteem leading to frustration with learning; overexposure to violence from television; racism; lack of employment opportunities; peer pressure; overcrowding; and other social, political, and bureaucratic factors that ignore the needs of the young (Hyman and D'Alessandro 1985).

What Is Discipline?

Discipline frequently is defined in terms of negative behavior, which requires some type of punishment to control it. A different, more positive view of discipline is provided by Hyman and D'Alessandro:

> But discipline in a democracy should spring from internal controls, not from fear of punishment. . . . Successful approaches to discipline in the schools enhance individual self-esteem and encourage cooperation. (1985)

Wayson defines discipline as:

> the ability to identify the character of a circumstance or situation to determine one's most constructive role in it, to carry out that role directly, to sustain it as long as necessary, and to learn from the consequences of one's actions. Such skill is learned; it is taught best by people who are willing to demonstrate it in their own lives. (1982)

If we accept Wayson's definition, then discipline is a skill resulting from training and practice in choosing behavior appropriate for a specific situation. The act of choosing implies that the best discipline is self-discipline.

Schools where students practice self-discipline have strong administrative leaders, who create an atmosphere that is "orderly without being rigid, quiet without being oppressive, and generally conducive to the instructional business at hand" (Edmonds 1979). Of equal importance, these administrators support intellectual and academic activities. They, the staff, and students hold a "shared vision" for schooling success (Edmond 1979; Furtwengler 1985). They enlist cooperation; therefore, they support and are supported by their staff (Wayson 1985).

Wayson has identified common characteristics in 500 well-disciplined schools he studied in the United States and Canada. He found the pervading environment in each of these schools was one where students had many opportunities to practice good discipline. The staffs of these schools:

- viewed their schools as places in which to do valuable, successful, and productive work;
- focused on causes of discipline problems rather than on the symptoms;
- emphasized positive and preventive practices, not punitive ones;
- adapted practices to meet their own needs and styles; and
- had faith in their students and themselves — and expended unusual amounts of energy to make their beliefs into realities. (Wayson 1985)

These schools promoted self-discipline through a wide variety of practices that can best be called good citizenship. To participate effectively in the political and social life of this country, students must learn and practice the skills needed by citizens in a democracy. These include the ability to interpret the basic workings of our government, to think productively about the improvement of society, to participate in large and small groups, and to involve oneself in resolving social problems (Goodlad 1979). Students are capable of self-discipline, but they must be taught "what it means to be a member of the society, how to behave toward others, what one's responsibilities are to the community and to the nation" (Bronfenbrenner 1986).

Learning the skills of human relations and civic responsibility can not be left to chance. Schools must plan programs deliberately for these purposes. Twenty-five years ago as a sixth-grade teacher in Cleveland, I began teaching good citizenship as a means of learning self-discipline. Our class motto was "We Practice Self-Discipline." Later, as an administrator in five elementary and middle schools, I broadened the classroom concept to a schoolwide program. These schools, with enrollments ranging from 300 to more than 1,000, served predominantly black students in one case, predominantly white students in three cases, and a racially mixed student body in the school described in this fastback. Students in each school represented a range of socioeconomic backgrounds.

In this fastback, I shall share a model of effective discipline involving democratic participation developed at the Prospect School in Oberlin, Ohio. While the model focuses on one elementary school, the practices described can be implemented in any elementary, intermediate, or middle school, regardless of the socioeconomic background or cultural differences of the student body.

Prospect School: A Profile

Prospect School is in the city of Oberlin, Ohio, 35 miles southwest of Cleveland. Oberlin's population of 9,512 includes 6,302 white citizens, 2,167 black, with the balance made up of Hispanic, Oriental, and American Indian. Employed in the city are 1,396 in managerial and professional occupations, 349 in executive and administrative jobs, and 993 in service occupations. Also, the community includes 431 persons earning less than $5,000 and 170 persons earning more than $50,000 annually (U.S. Census 1980). The largest employer in the city is Oberlin College, a private institution founded more than 150 years ago, with 850 employees.

Prospect School is situated on a tree-lined street in the midst of this well-established residential area. Originally built in 1887, it has had four additions in the past 76 years; the latest, in 1981, modernized the one-and-a-half story facility inside and out. It currently houses grades three through five and serves all students in those grades in the Oberlin City School System. Students living beyond a two-mile radius are bused to the school. Enrollment in 1985-86 was 319 students, with 57.4% white, 39.5% black, 0.9% Hispanic, 1.3% Oriental, and 0.9% American Indian. There are four classes of each grade level, which are organized heterogeneously. Three are open classrooms, two team-teaching, and the rest are self-contained.

The staff includes 12 full-time classroom teachers; three special subject teachers for art, music, and physical education; one Chapter One reading teacher; one teacher for the developmentally handicapped; two reading resource unit teachers; and two part-time tutors for students with learning disabilities. One teacher is Oriental; the others are white. The principal is black. The average years of teaching experience of the teaching staff is 14.3 years.

In terms of its demographics and organizational structure, Prospect School is similar to thousands of elementary schools. But it also has something extra. Read on.

Prospect School's Model for Effective Discipline

Our program for school discipline began with the preparation of a philosophy statement for Prospect School. At our initial staff meeting in the fall of 1984, I asked for volunteers to serve on the philosophy committee. The committee met several times and received input from the others on the staff. The draft of the philosophy statement was given to every member of the staff, first to critique, then to accept or reject. There was unanimous acceptance of the philosophy statement, and it was published in the school newsletter sent to parents and the community.

The Prospect School Philosophy is brief; its language is simple so it can be readily understood by even the youngest students. It speaks to students, parents, teachers, and the principal. It reads as follows:

We believe that:

- Each and every student should get the best education possible.
- Students should come to school prepared to participate in the learning activities.
- Students should respect the teachers.
- Parents should see that the students get adequate rest and nutriment.

- Parents should communicate with the teachers and principal.
- Teachers should be prepared to teach every day.
- Teachers should respect the students.
- Teachers should communicate often with parents.
- The principal should facilitate the educational program and support the teachers.
- The principal should communicate with parents.

Having a school philosophy tells the staff, students, parents, and community what our mission is; it serves as a reference and gives a sense of shared purpose for all; and it delegates responsibility to all parties concerned — students, parents, teachers, and the principal.

One of our goals identified for providing students the "best education possible" was to give them a sense of responsibility and the autonomy to exercise that responsibility. If students are to learn how to exercise self-discipline, they need opportunities to plan and manage certain of their school activities — activities that provide them with models of good citizenship behavior.

I explained to the staff my experience with using the student council concept for teaching responsibility and self-discipline. Through a variety of committees and clubs, students would have many opportunities to learn to practice responsibility and self-discipline. The staff agreed that they, too, should model the kinds of behavior we expected of our students.

We began with separate meetings with each grade level of the school at which I introduced the student council concept and explained how it related to good citizenship. They accepted the concept readily because I told them they would get to make up the school rules. If we expect students to follow school rules, then having them make the rules provides the best assurance that they will be followed.

The next step was for each of the 12 homerooms to form a Homeroom Club and elect a president, vice president, secretary, and two room representatives to attend weekly Student Council meetings. After several meetings with the room representatives to draft a Student Council Constitution, it was time to nominate candidates for Student Council officers for the whole school. Those nominated wrote short campaign speeches, which they delivered over the public address system and on a tour of the homerooms. The candidates went as a group to each room during the time between the students' arrival in the morning and the start of instruction (usually 15 minutes). The students made posters and campaign buttons at home. Campaigning was limited to three days. Election was by secret ballot. Oberlin's chief of police accepted my invitation to install the new officers. He presented each student a certificate with his or her name, school, and office held in the Student Council. For an extra touch, each certificate carried the official seal of the City of Oberlin.

The participation of the police chief in a ceremonial function is one small yet impressive example of community involvement in our citizenship program. Of greater significance is how we secured extensive parent and community involvement to reinforce what we were attempting to do at Prospect School.

As the school year began in 1984, a great amount of administrative time was being devoted to student-student and student-teacher conflicts. There were student fights at the bus stops, quarrels on the bus and playground, and talking back rudely to teachers. These problems were recurring across the school system at all grade levels. Parents and the community needed to be aware of these kinds of behavior at school.

After discussing my concern about the problem behavior with our superintendent, I designed a survey questionnaire to collect data for two purposes: 1) to investigate what are the major behavior problems of some Oberlin students, and 2) to raise the awareness level of the parents and community concerning these problems. My fellow administrators at the other three Oberlin City schools were as interested as I was to see the responses to the survey.

The questionnaire was distributed to each student in the school system to take home to parents and was also available in local drug stores, banks, and the library. In addition, teachers throughout the system and students in grades five, seven, nine, and eleven received the questionnaire. There were 792 questionnaires returned, with 339 from parents, 58 from community members, 35 from teachers, and 360 from students.

A committee of 19 volunteers comprised of community members, parents, school personnel (teachers, administrators, counselors, and psychologist), and two students from each grade level that was surveyed analyzed the data. This committee recommended an evening community meeting to report the findings. The large attendance at the meeting demonstrated the community's interest.

Some of the findings of the Oberlin Schools Survey were:

1. The three biggest behavior problems at school are threats to other students, disrespect shown to teachers, and fighting.

2. The main reason given for disciplinary problems in school is that "students lack proper discipline training."

3. To improve students' overall social behavior, the school needs to establish closer relations with parents or guardians.

The Oberlin Schools Survey succeeded in raising the awareness of the total community about behavior problems and the need for discipline training. And one direct result was the founding of the Prospect Parent Teachers Association, which proved to be an excellent vehicle for improving communications between our school and the home.

The Prospect PTA came to be a strong supporter of our school discipline program. It encouraged our School Spirit Day held every week with the sale of Prospect Panther T-Shirts. It sponsored an essay contest that involved students in research about the Statue of Liberty and also contests in song writing and art. It sponsored an old-fashioned spelling bee that challenged students to study above and beyond their regular assignments.

Starting our school discipline program required a lot of hard work during its first year at Prospect in 1984-85. Total involvement of students, staff, and parents made it work. In the next section we shall look at how it works.

"We shall kick off the campaign with a march beginning inside and ending outside the building, where we shall all join hands making a circle around the building. Also, we shall have Adopt-A-Friend. And every present Good Citizen can choose someone who hasn't made it yet to be a friend."

When Sonja concluded her report, the audience applauded enthusiastically. The children obviously were excited in anticipation of the Campaign for Good Citizenship.

Next, Heidi asked if there was any new business, the fourth item on her agenda. There being none, she called on the vice president, Kim, a fourth-grader, to announce the committee or club reports and to invite each chairperson to come up and present the report.

Judge of Student Court, Terrel

"Thank you, Kim. I am sorry to say that there was one case in court this month for fighting. We remind you that when you get angry, then you fight. Just be very slow to anger, and you can prevent fighting."

Radio Club, Carissa and Dale

"Thank you, Kim. This month, we had 62 fourth-graders participate in the morning broadcast. We commemorated Brotherhood Month. We give a special thank you to all who shared some information about an outstanding American who contributed to making our country great. Dale?"

"Next month, we'll begin with announcers from third grade. Also, emember to bring in can goods for the county Hunger Task Force rive. A box will be placed in the front hall on Monday. Your ideas ɛ important. If you wish to share them with us, just write them down th your name and homeroom number and give them to our school retary in the office. We are always looking for ways to improve broadcasts and our school. Thank you."

logy Club, Jennifer

'hank you, Kim. This month the Ecology Club planted tulip and cinth bulbs in front of the building. Also, we thank all of the nts who assisted us with picking up paper on the playground af- ɛ picnic last Wednesday."

Prospect School's Discipline Program in Action

It was the last day of the month, and the entire student body of Prospect School, along with their teachers and some parent visitors assembled in the multipurpose room for the monthly Student Council meeting.

Heidi, a fifth-grader and president of Student Council, rapped gavel and said, "I call this meeting to order. Let us stand to sa Pledge of Allegiance to our flag and sing one verse of 'Ameri Beautiful'."

She had asked the music teacher beforehand to accompany ing at the piano. Following the singing, she asked the au be seated. On the table before her was an agenda she ha to guide her as she led the business portion of the mee

"Now let us have the secretary's minutes of the last n nounced Heidi. Fifth-grader Chelonn stood up and rea from the Student Council weekly meeting held the p in the library. At the weekly meetings only the home tatives, officers, committee/club chairpersons, the entire homeroom (a different one each week) are

Heidi then called for old or unfinished busine

Sonja, a third-grader, reported on the progres forthcoming Campaign for Good Citizenship.

Safety Patrol Captain, Tameka

"Thank you, Kim. First of all, we would like to give a big hand to the third-graders for their cooperation with the patrols in the third-grade hall. But I am sorry to say that some of the fourth-graders are banging their locker doors shut. We ask that you lift the handle when you close the door. Try it, it works. Thank you."

The Perspective Editor, Rachel

"Thank you, Kim. We apologize that the paper came out a little late this month. However, next month's issue will be right on time, and we know that you'll enjoy it. Besides homeroom news, we'll have a special interview with one of our teachers."

Health Committee, Shira

"Thank you, Kim," said Shira, the only third-grader making a standing committee report. "This month the Health Committee took a field trip to the County Health Department. We learned about some of the health problems of the human body. Here are Jean, Sherman, Jason, and Shane to tell you about them."

As these children presented their brief reports, they used drawings of the body to illustrate their points.

Each student making a report at the Student Council meeting writes it out, with the help of the committee or club advisor, if necessary. The student practices reading the report before delivering it at Student Council. Each student receives applause from the audience after the report is given.

Heidi thanked vice president Kim and the chairpersons for the reports and went on to the next item on her agenda, special recognitions.

Special Recognitions

There is always a place on the agenda for recognizing student achievements, awards, or any worthwhile deed performed in or out of school. The presentation may be made by a teacher, parent, or member of the community. Today was no exception. Heidi introduced Mrs. Sheldorsky, the City Recreation Center director, who presented certificates of merit to Ken and Raymond for their entries in a poster contest about home safety. Next, Heidi called on the advisor of the Safety Patrol to present an award to the outstanding patrol of the month. Alan came forward to receive the gold badge that he will wear until the next monthly meeting of Student Council. The audience applauded Alan.

Recognition of Good Citizens

When Heidi announces that the principal will now award certificates to this month's new Good Citizens, a hush comes over the assembly. Although the students who will receive Good Citizen awards today know who they are, they always approach this portion of the assembly as though it is a secret to be uncovered. The students listen attentively for their homeroom number and their teacher's announcement of those students who have followed the rules of good citizenship and practiced self-discipline this month. As the teacher calls the name of the student to be recognized for the first time, the student goes up on the stage; the principal congratulates the student and presents a certificate that says the student consistently has displayed self-discipline. Heidi gives each student a ribbon that reads, "Prospect Panthers Are Number One." The ribbon has a piece of yarn attached so it can be worn around the neck like an Olympic medal.

Also, the teachers call the names of those students who have received a certificate and ribbon in previous months and who continue to display self-discipline. These students stand in place and receive applause from the audience. The number of students receiving recognition as Good Citizens varies from room to room and from month to month. There is no set number allowed.

The significance the Good Citizen award holds for students is illustrated in the following case.

Tania, a fifth-grader, had recently transferred to Prospect from another city. She started off at Prospect on the "wrong foot." She poked fun at others, used vulgar language and name-calling, and told lies for why her assignments were not done. Her behavior caused the other girls in her class to ostracize her.

About this time, cheerleader tryouts were being held. The only requirements for tryouts were to be in fifth grade and to audition on the stage by singing, dancing, or telling a joke. But most of the students preferred to try out with a cheer, since the cheerleaders performed at every monthly Student Council meeting and all the students knew the cheers.

Tania came to the tryouts, did her cheer, and was so good she impressed all the students. When it came time to vote in new members, the cheerleaders were reluctant to accept Tania because of her past history of causing trouble. The captain reminded her that in order to perform and to stay on the team, a cheerleader must display good citizenship. But Tania was voted in, and it seemed to make a world of difference in her school life.

Cheerleading practice was every Tuesday and Thursday during lunch recess. Tania was always there and appeared to be getting along well with the others. But the week prior to the monthly Student Council meeting, she got into trouble, didn't get on the Good Citizen list, and therefore wasn't eligible to perform. Outwardly her first reaction was to be negative, but the cheerleader advisor knew she was only covering up her true feelings. The advisor reminded her that if being a cheerleader meant so much to her, she knew what she had to do.

This month Tania made it. When her teacher called her name for the award, Tania had to fight back tears as she made her way to the stage. Everyone gave her a big applause. This was indeed her victory!

After the last homeroom's Good Citizens are recognized, president Heidi adjourns the meeting and vice president Kim introduces the program. Each homeroom takes turns preparing a 15- to 20-minute program to conclude the monthly Student Council meeting. This month a fifth-grade class had prepared a choral reading of "Casey at the Bat," under the direction of their teacher and a friend of the teacher who lives in the community.

Generally, the monthly meeting of Student Council is an hour long; including the program. The smaller weekly meetings are about 25-minutes long; the weekly meetings are devoted to airing school problems of a general interest to the student body and to resolving specific classroom problems.

Making Rules and Living by Them

The Prospect School Student Council operates under a constitution that is loosely patterned after our U.S. Constitution. It has a preamble, articles, and sections. It is a simple document written by children for children. It is theirs. They are responsible for it; they are responsible to it. It provides both guidelines for student behavior and a structure for carrying out a variety of activities that contribute to good citizenship and self-discipline.

The Good Citizen rules, which appear in Article I, Section 1, were developed by the student representatives with the help of the Student Council advisor. Before they became a part of the constitution, every student at Prospect was given a copy to study and discuss in homeroom and to take home and discuss with parents. The students agreed that a three-fourths majority was needed to ratify the constitution. The vote was taken a week later.

Below is the text of the constitution. The specifics may not be appropriate for every school, but it is a model that works at Prospect School.

Constitution of the
Prospect School Student Council

Preamble: We the students of Prospect School, hereby establish our Student Council in order to promote the development of self-discipline and good citizenship in each and every student.

Article I: Eligibility for Membership

Section 1 — A Good Citizen:
1. Knows and obeys classroom, school, and bus rules.
2. Follows safety rules and obeys the Safety Patrol.
3. Shows self-respect.
4. Is kind and courteous to others.
5. Always tries to do his/her best work (has good work habits).
6. Is responsible for his/her own behavior.
7. Tries to prevent fighting.

8. Is honest and fair.
9. Practices good health habits.
10. Tries not to pollute.

When a student is displaying the 10 rules of a good citizen, he/she is practicing self-discipline.

Section 2 — Homeroom Club

Each homeroom shall have a club that holds a meeting every week of the month to determine the good citizens for the week. Students will be nominated by other students, or students may nominate themselves. Any student may disagree with any nomination and must state a truthful reason for disagreeing. The homeroom members will vote on each nominee based on the above rules for a good citizen. Homeroom Club shall have a president, secretary, and any other officer necessary. The president shall preside at the meetings.

Section 3 — Recognition of Good Citizens of the Month

At the end of the month, students who have been on the homeroom club's good citizens list every week of the month will be recognized at the monthly Student Council meeting by our principal.

Article II — Operating Procedure

Section 1 — Power for Making Rules

All rule-making power of the Prospect Student Council will be given to the officers thereof and to the principal of Prospect School. Election of officers will be by secret ballot and will take place during the first six weeks of each school year in the fall. Students in grades three through five will vote for all officers to be elected.

Section 2 — President

The qualifications of the President will be that he or she is in the fifth grade, is a good citizen, is responsible, and has good behavior and self-discipline. This position will be held for the entire school year. The President will preside over all meetings of Council.

Section 3 — Vice President

The qualifications of the Vice President will be that he or she is in the fourth grade, is a good citizen, is responsible, and has good behavior and self-discipline. This position will be held for the entire school year. The Vice President will oversee the reporting of activities by the various committees and clubs at the monthly Student Council meetings.

Section 4 — Secretary

The qualifications of the Secretary will be that he or she is in the fifth grade, is good in spelling and English, has good behavior, is responsible, and has self-discipline. This position will be held for the entire school year. The Secretary will write the minutes and read them at each Council meeting, and will take attendance by calling the roll at each weekly meeting.

Section 5 — Treasurer

The qualifications of the Treasurer will be that he or she is in any grade, has good behavior, is responsible, is good in math, and has self-discipline. The Treasurer will be appointed by the President with the approval of the student body, as the need arises for such a position. This position, once appointed, may be held for the entire school year.

Section 6 — Judge of Student Court

The qualifications of the Judge will be that he or she is in the fourth or fifth grade, is a good citizen, is responsible, has good behavior, is honest and fair, and has self-discipline. The Judge will preside over Student Court and give sentencing to students found guilty of breaking rules. The Judge can never sentence a student to corporal punishment.

Article III — Authorized Standing Committees

Section 1 — Health Committee

The purpose of the Health Committee will be to promote good health and safety habits for the entire student body. The Committee will be made up of students in third through fifth grade with one member from each homeroom. A second member from the same homeroom will serve as the alternate. The chairperson of the Health Committee can be selected from the committee members, by the President of Student Council, or elected by the committee members at the discretion of the President. The chairperson will preside over the meetings. The committee and the advisor will determine what issues to cover in the best interest of the student body of Prospect School. The Health Committee will present lessons about good health and/or safety at each Student Council meeting once a month, make posters on safety and health issues, arrange for resource persons for assemblies, and plan other activities in the best interest of the Prospect student body.

Section 2 — Safety Patrol

The purpose of the Safety Patrol will be to promote and enforce safety and self-discipline for the entire student body of Prospect School. The members of the Safety Patrol will be fourth- and fifth-graders and will be good citizens. There will be one captain and one fourth-grade lieutenant and one fifth-grade lieutenant. The captain and the lieutenants will be chosen by the other patrol members. Members will be assigned guard posts by the advisor. The captain will be responsible for making daily checks to see that posts are covered. The captain may place a substitute on an uncovered post from members who do not have an assignment. Should there be no one to cover a post, the captain may assign a lieutenant or report the matter to the advisor. The captain and lieutenants will serve as a committee to report to the weekly Student Council any problems relating to the safety or welfare of the student body.

Section 3 — Radio Club

The purpose of the Radio Club is to give the Prospect student body a chance to participate in delivering the morning announcements and daily broadcasts. At least twice a school year each homeroom will be asked to send three students to the office ten minutes before the start of school to practice for the ten-minute broadcast. Students are asked to prepare a weather report for the day, a report on a current event, or an item of special interest, such as a book report, poems, jokes, etc. These students will make the broadcast that day. The students will take turns broadcasting so that all who wish to can participate. The chairperson and co-chairperson will be selected by the advisor and will alternate weekly so that one is in attendance every day of a given week. These students will be fifth-graders.

Section 4 — Ecology Club

The purpose of the Ecology Club is to promote a clean school environment, inside and outside. There will be a representative chosen from each homeroom to serve for the entire school year. Ecology Club will have projects at least twice a semester to help the student body to learn about the ecology and to beautify Prospect School. The chairperson will be elected by the members of the club. The chairperson will preside over all meetings.

Article IV — Authorized Activities

Section 1 — Good Citizens of the Month

There will be recognition of Good Citizens of the Month during the schoolwide Student Council meeting held each month in the multipurpose room or in another location announced by the principal. Good Citizens of the Month will be presented with a token of esteem indicating their membership in the Prospect School Student Council one time during the school year. The following items, for example, may be presented to the student: a certificate, a button, or a T-shirt.

Section 2 — Other Activities

During the school year, students may suggest other activities that involve the Prospect student body. Any activity for and by the students may be approved by a majority vote of the students and with the approval of the Prospect faculty and principal.

An example of how one part of the constitution is implemented is described below. The Student Court is made up of the judge, the bailiff (student receiving the second highest number of votes for judge), one juror from each of the 12 homerooms, the defendants, their witnesses, and the principal. A foreman of the jury is selected by the jurors during their deliberation of the case. There are no spectators.

The principal, who also serves as the Student Council advisor, handles all serious disciplinary problems, not the Student Court. The Student Court is convened only at the discretion of the principal. Since students give up their lunch recess to participate in Student Court, it usually is not convened more than once a week, if then.

The defendants receive subpoenas the morning of the day court will convene. During the morning broadcast, it is announced that Student Court will convene at a specified time and room. And homerooms are asked to send jurors.

The following is a scenario of a typical Student Court session.

Bailiff: Hear ye, hear ye, This court is now in session. The Honorable Judge Terrel Dampier presiding. All rise.

Judge: (Raps his gavel twice on table.) Please be seated. This court will hear the case of Cirel Yonek and Tower Campbell, charged with violating Good Citizens Rule 7, fighting each other. Cirel, how do you plead? Guilty or not guilty.

Cirel: Not guilty.

Judge: Tower, how do you plead? Guilty or not guilty.

Tower: Not guilty.

Judge: You may each tell your side. Cirel.

(Cirel tells what he thinks happened.)

Judge: Jurors, do you have any questions?

(The members of the jury ask questions of the defendant to get a better understanding of what took place.)

Judge: Cirel, are there any witnesses to what happened?

(If there are witnesses, the judge will allow each to speak. Jurors also may ask them questions.)

Judge: Tower, you may now tell your side.

(The same procedure is followed with questions from jurors and witnesses.)

Judge: Jury, you have heard the testimonies of this case. Please deliberate the evidence presented. Find the defendants guilty as charged, one guilty, one not guilty, or both not guilty.

(The jurors go out into the hall, select a foreman, and discuss the case. When they reach a verdict, they re-enter the room and take their seats.)

Judge: Foreman of the jury, have you and the other jurors reached a verdict?

Foreman: Yes, we have, your Honor. We find Cirel guilty and Tower not guilty.

Judge: Thank you, jury. Cirel, you are to stay in the next three days during lunch recess. You are to write a two-page report on what injuries are caused by fighting. You may go to the library to do your report. The work must be neat and the words spelled correctly. If not, you will have to do it over during lunch recess until it is acceptable.

Judge: (Raps his gavel.) Court is adjourned.

Components of the Model

To some, the Prospect School Student Council might be considered an extracurricular activity, since it occurs outside the classroom instructional program. We regard it as a vital part of our overall educational plan, which includes teaching self-discipline and promoting good citizenship. The components of our model include those identified in research on well-disciplined schools. These components fall under four main headings: 1) a shared sense of purpose for discipline training, 2) focus on the individual student's needs, 3) purposeful and organized activity for learning self-discipline, and 4) personal responsibility for success of the program. The following discussion of each of these components is intended to help administrators and teachers who wish to design their own program.

A Shared Sense of Purpose for Discipline Training

This model requires that every member of the staff support and contribute to the goal of promoting and developing self-discipline and good citizenship in all students. Furthermore, it assumes that all students can learn self-discipline and good citizenship if given the appropriate environment and the right opportunities.

An essential aspect of the school environment is how the adults there interact with each other and with the students. How students interpret the behaviors and attitudes of these significant adults will determine to a large extent the kind of discipline that prevails. All adults must be models of the behavior they expect the students to display. As John Dewey said, "We never educate directly, but indirectly by means of the environment."

The key person who establishes a shared sense of purpose for the school discipline program is the principal. This person must believe in the program, convey its objectives, and suggest ways of carrying them out. The principal sets the leadership tone by modeling the desired behaviors for the staff and the students. The principal delegates leadership to staff and students and supports them in carrying out their roles.

The staff also have a vital role in creating a shared sense of purpose. This is demonstrated in the support they give to the principal and in the atmosphere they create in the classroom to foster self-discipline and good citizenship. By allocating time for a student-governed Homeroom Club, the teachers are providing opportunities for all students to learn and perform skills needed for democratic participation in the governance of the school. When misbehavior occurs, the teachers do not respond with sarcasm or ridicule; they allow students to evaluate their behavior according to a set of standards adopted by the student body.

Still another key person on the discipline training team is the staff member who serves as the Student Council advisor. This person is the liaison between the Student Council and the staff. The advisor must be an effective teacher in order to guide the Student Council members in their various roles and in their working relationships with each other. By exhibiting positive leadership behaviors, the advisor serves as an example to the Student Council members as they exercise their authority over school activities.

Focus on the Individual Student's Needs

When students are involved in self-directed activities under the supervision of the Student Council advisor, they gain self-confidence. They come to see their school as a place where they can make things happen. Many student needs are met through their involvement in the activities of the Student Council. It provides:

- activities for both small groups and the whole student body.
- opportunities to develop responsibility, initiative, and leadership skills.
- a simplified yet basic understanding of how a democratic government works.
- a vehicle for communicating student concerns to school authorities.
- opportunities to learn respect for differences of opinion.

As students come to understand the need for rules and have a role in making and enforcing those rules, they are on the road to developing self-discipline and good citizenship.

Purposeful and Organized Activity for Learning Self-Discipline

Every activity has the ultimate goal of fostering self-discipline. All activities take place during the school day and are under adult supervision.

In addition to the committees and clubs described in the Student Council constitution, there is School Spirit Day every Thursday. Students wear clothing with the school's colors, red and blue. Teachers, too, often join in the spirit of things and wear red and blue on this day. During homeroom in the morning, a count is taken of the number of students wearing red and blue. There are always ties for the homerooms in first place, second place, and honorable mention, thus many homerooms receive recognition.

At Thursday morning Radio Club, the homeroom awards for school spirit are announced, the students applaud, and the homerooms receive a certificate with the Prospect Panther emblem on it. Selecting the school's colors and the black panther as the school mascot were decisions the students voted on.

During the winter when inclement weather prevents outdoor recess, activities are planned to involve the whole school. One such activity was Fun Day, which was scheduled in the afternoon in place of the normal schedule. Every teacher sponsored an activity, in some cases with another teacher. The activities included handicrafts, games, arts, cooking, and candy making. The principal led a cheerleading session. Students could select three activities and move from one to another on their own. Much fun was had by all.

Another winter activity was an Indoor Picnic. The students invited their families to the school on this day during the lunch hour. Planning the event with the help of the food service staff took about three weeks. A nutritious box lunch was prepared at the same cost as the regular school lunch. Orders were taken for the lunch up to three days before the picnic. Students on the free federal lunch program received a free box lunch; guests were charged the regular amount. The desks were pushed aside in the classroom by the students and teachers to create the "picnic grounds." Parents, grandparents, uncles, aunts, and neighbors came 480 strong!

Fun Day and the Indoor Picnic are examples of Authorized Activities in the Prospect School Student Council constitution.

Personal Responsibility for the Success of the Program

Responsibility for the discipline in the school ultimately rests with the principal and the teachers. However, the real issue is not who is responsible for discipline in the school, but rather what *kind* of discipline should there be in the school. Our program at Prospect School makes the principal and teachers' jobs easier, because it is based on the kind of activities that help students become self-disciplined, self-directed American citizens. We invite you to try our model.

References

Austin, G. "Exemplary Schools and the Search for Effectiveness." *Educational Leadership* (October 1979): 10-14.

Baker, K. "Research Evidence of a School Discipline Problem." *Phi Delta Kappan* (March 1985): 482-88.

Bauer, G.L. "Restoring Order to the Public Schools." *Phi Delta Kappan* (March 1985): 488-91.

Bronfenbrenner, U. "Alienation and the Four Worlds of Childhood." *Phi Delta Kappan* (February 1986): 430-36.

Edmonds, R. "Effective Schools for the Urban Poor." *Educational Leadership* (October 1979): 15-23.

Furtwengler, W.J. "Implementing Strategies for A School Effectiveness Program." *Phi Delta Kappan* (December 1985): 262-65.

Goodlad, J.I. *What Schools Are For.* Bloomington, Ind: Phi Delta Kappa Educational Foundation, 1979.

Huckaby, W.O. "Integrating Style and Purpose in Leadership." *Educational Leadership* (May 1980): 613-16.

Hyman, I.A., and D'Alessandro, J. "Good Old-Fashioned Discipline: The Politics of Punitiveness." *Phi Delta Kappan* (September 1984): 39-45.

Scott, R., and Walberg, H.J. "Schools Alone Are Insufficient." *Educational Leadership* (October 1979): 24-27.

Thomason, J., and Pedersen, J. "A School Discipline Alternative: A Program for a Junior High School." *Education Digest* (April 1985): 54-56.

U.S. Bureau of the Census for 1980 of Lorain County, Ohio, Oberlin Tract. Available in the office of the City Manager, Oberlin, Ohio.

Wayson, W. "Creating Schools That Teach Self-Discipline" Phi Delta Kappa Educational Foundation Workshop Manual. Bloomington, Ind: Phi Delta Kappa International, 1982.

Wayson, W. "The Politics of Violence in School: Doublespeak and Disruptions in Public Confidence." *Phi Delta Kappan* (October 1985): 127-32.